THE MEGA BOOK OF
3-D THRILLERS!
AMAZING EYE-POPPING EXPERIENCES

ARCTURUS

ARCTURUS

This edition published in 2010 by Arcturus Publishing Limited
26/27 Bickels Yard, 151–153 Bermondsey Street,
London SE1 3HA

ISBN: 978-1-84837-250-4
CH000510EN
Supplier 03, Date 0610, Print run 198

Printed in China

CONTENTS

DINOSAURS

Millions and millions of years before any people lived on Earth, the world belonged to the dinosaurs. These amazing creatures first appeared about 228 million years ago. These magnificent beasts ranged in size from the knee-high to the sky-high, and ruled the Earth for about 160 million years. Humans have only been around for about 1.5 million years, so we have quite a lot of catching up to do!

DINOSAUR DAYS

Dinosaurs lived during the Mesozoic Era, which began 245 million years ago and ended 65 million years ago. Each of three periods in the Mesozoic Era had its own cool creatures. The Triassic Period (248–206 million years ago) gave us the earliest dinosaurs, like *Herrerasaurus* (eh-ray-rah-SORE-us), as well as the first small mammals. The Jurassic Period (206–142 million years ago) produced plant-eaters like *Stegosaurus* (steg-oh-SORE-us) and meat-eaters like *Allosaurus* (al-oh-SORE-us). And the Cretaceous Period (142–65 million years ago) was the time of *Iguanadon* (ig-WHA-noh-don) and *Deinonychus* (die-NON-i-kus) and, sadly, the end of the line for the dinosaurs.

▼ EMPTY NESTERS

Like most reptiles, dinosaurs laid and hatched from eggs. For many years, palaeontologists (scientists who study prehistoric life) thought that dinosaurs were pretty relaxed parents, to put it mildly: in their tough neighbourhood, maybe self-preservation was considered a higher priority than taking care of the children! But some fossils now indicate that certain dinosaurs may have been very protective of their young, like one Cretaceous plant-eater who apparently guarded its babies and brought them food. Palaeontologists named this dinosaur *Maiasaura* (my-ah-SORE-ah), or 'good mother lizard'.

▲ CAN YOU DIG IT?

When most dinosaurs died, their bodies just rotted away and nothing remained of them. But if a dinosaur died and the conditions were right, the bones would gradually become petrified (turned to stone). By examining these ancient remains, called fossils, palaeontologists can learn what a dinosaur looked like, how it moved, and what – or who! – it ate for dinner.

Scientists believe that there are hundreds of dinosaur species yet to be found. You might make the next big discovery!

Mighty Meat

Carnivorous dinosaurs, the most fearsome, wouldn't have won any popularity contests. Some, like the recently discovered Giganotosaurus (JI-gah-NO-tuh-SORE-us), were humongous, but there were also mini meat-munchers like **Compsognathus** (komp-soh-NAY-thus), which was no bigger than a modern chicken. But they all had the same favourite meal: meat — and the tools to get it. When their dagger-like, flesh-ripping teeth fell or wore out, new ones grew in to take their place. No dentures for these dudes!

Palaeontologists can learn what dinosaurs ate by examining fossils called coprolites – the scientific name for dino dung.

▲ RUN FOR YOUR LIFE!

Some of the most dangerous carnivorous dinosaurs were small but speedy – and well-armed! Deinonychus was only 3.5 metres long, but fast and fierce. Its name, which means 'terrible claw', refers to the long, curved claw on each of its back feet, which it used to slash its prey. It also had a relatively big brain – bad news for its intended victims.

Eaters

FOOD FIGHTS ▶

While some herbivorous (plant-eating) dinosaurs may have been gentle, they didn't necessarily give up without a struggle. In Mongolia's Gobi Desert, the bones of a meat-eating *Velociraptor* (vel-O-si-RAP-tor, meaning 'speedy robber') and the bones of a plant-eating *Protoceratops* (pro-toe-SER-a-tops) were found together, indicating a fight to the finish – for both of them. So much for fast food!

▼ ARMED AND DANGEROUS

At under 11 metres long, Allosaurus was the top predator of the Jurassic Period. It had a powerful tail, three strong claws on each hand, and a mouthful of teeth with jagged edges perfect for tearing and chewing flesh. You wouldn't hear this diner complain that his meat was too tough!

The great meat-eater Megalosaurus (MEG-ah-loh-SORE-us), or 'great reptile', was the first dinosaur ever to be named. When its leg bone was unearthed, people first thought they had discovered the remains of a giant man.

Herbivores: Gen

The biggest creatures that have ever walked the Earth were the herbivorous (plant-eating) dinosaurs. Just the neck of the Mamenchisaurus (mah-MEN-chee-SORE-us) measured 12 metres long — the length of a bus. Another long-neck, Seismosaurus (SIZE-moh-sore-us), may have measured nearly 40 metres. That's the length of two bowling alley lanes! The plant-eaters went looking for food, not trouble, so other dinosaurs had little to fear from them. But a meat-eater that provoked or attacked them might get more than it bargained for.

▲ **VEGETARIAN VENGEANCE**

Imagine long-necked reptiles the height of six men standing on each other's shoulders and as heavy as a dozen elephants! *Brachiosaurus* (brak-ee-oh-SORE-us) was way too massive to move fast. But it had a thick and powerful tail, great for whacking Jurassic attackers like *Allosaurus* and *Ceratosaurus* (seh-rat-oh-SORE-us). And while its thick, tree-like limbs weren't built for speed, Brachiosaurus might have been able to rear back on its hind legs and crash its front ones down on its enemy. Take that!

◄ **TOUGH LOVE**

The plant-eating *Pachycephalosaurus* (PAK-ee-SEF-a-loh-SORE-us) was a real bonehead! The solid dome on the top of its skull was 25 centimetres thick. Some scientists believe that during the mating season, rival males would fight for females by charging at each other headfirst. Those built-in crash helmets certainly came in handy.

TLE GiaNts?

▼ WEAPONS OR WEATHERPROOFING?

The strange-looking *Stegosaurus* has long puzzled palaeontologists. Most now agree that its triangular plates formed a row down its back and served as a sort of prehistoric furnace *and* air-conditioner. Stegosaurus may have turned its plates towards the sun to soak in rays to warm its body, while a breeze through the plates would cool it down. Scientists used to think that the plates discouraged predators from snacking on Stegosaurus, but further study has revealed that they weren't really too sturdy. Fortunately, the one-metre-long, spear-like spikes on its tail would have been excellent weapons.

Poor Stegosaurus has another claim to fame besides its weird appearance: Its walnut-sized brain was smaller than any other dinosaur's.

The Polished pebbles found among some plant-eating dinosaur remains suggest that before they gulped down their leafy lunches, some dinosaurs may have swallowed stones to help grind up their food.

Tyrannosaurus:

When you hear the word 'dinosaur', what comes to mind first? Bet you said T. rex! **Tyrannosaurus rex (tie-RAN-oh-SORE-us REX)**, whose name means 'king of the tyrant lizards', was definitely one of the biggest, hungriest and fiercest meat-eating dinosaurs. Standing 6 metres tall and 13 metres long, it had massive hind legs and huge, powerful jaws – and an appetite to match! Amazingly, in 1993, palaeontologists unearthed another carnivorous dinosaur that seems to have been even bigger and fiercer than Tyrannosaurus. Still, T. rex will always loom large in every dino fan's imagination.

▶ TYRANT OR TRASH CAN?

T. rex certainly had the equipment of a killing machine. But some scientists argue that with its huge bulk and short arms, which were probably useless for catching prey, Tyrannosaurus was probably not the most efficient of hunters. It may have got most of its meals by feeding on sick or wounded dinosaurs – or even by eating the remains of prey killed by other carnivores. Imagine: a king eating leftovers!

The Ex-Rex?

It would have taken about 290 teachers a year to keep a Tyrannosaurus Rex fed!

SUPER REX

In 1990, one of the largest and most complete Tyrannosaurus skeletons ever unearthed was found in South Dakota, USA. Named 'Sue', after its discoverer, this fossilized dinosaur was a real tough customer. A number of its bones had been broken but had rehealed over time. The broken bones were probably a result of fierce battles with other T. rex.

▲ ALL THE BETTER TO EAT YOU WITH

Tyrannosaurus rex was certainly a bigmouth! With a head as long as a refrigerator, it could have opened its jaws wide enough to swallow a man in one gulp. Curved, jagged teeth, longer than a human hand, could puncture its prey's organs before tearing it apart. T. rex's teeth were made for ripping, not chewing, so it had to swallow each mouthful whole. What dreadful table manners!

THE RIGHTFUL KING ▶

Giganotosaurus, whose name means 'giant lizard of the south', was discovered in Argentina in 1993. When this dinosaur's skull and thigh bone measured bigger than Sue's, it became clear that *Tyrannosaurus* was *rex* no more! How long will *Giganotosaurus* be number 1? Its reign could end at any time, since new types of dinosaurs are being found every year. But until then – Long Live the King!

The Real Sea

While dinosaurs roamed the Earth, equally awesome beasts ruled the seas. Many of these oceanic monsters evolved from land reptiles and adapted to life in the water. But though some looked pretty fishy, they were still reptiles, and had to come to the water's surface to breathe between dives, like whales and dolphins do. The prehistoric sea monsters came in all shapes and sizes. Some had long necks and flippers, while others had long jaws filled with razor-sharp teeth. One of the biggest, Kronosaurus (KRON-oh-SORE-us), with its 2.5-metre head, feasted on prehistoric squids, sharks — and its fellow seafaring reptiles!

Beautifully preserved fossils suggest that Ichthyosaurs didn't lay eggs but gave birth to their little ones live in the water.

▼ GONE FISHIN'

Ichthyosaurs (IKH-thee-oh-sores), like this 15-metre-long *Shonisaurus* (shon-ee-SORE-us), were the super swimmers of the prehistoric seas. They looked and lived a lot like modern-day dolphins – but they were much, much bigger. With their sleek bodies, back fins, and strong tails, the Ichthyosaurs zipped through the water as fast as 40 kmph. When their big eyes spotted a tasty meal, their long, tooth-lined jaws would open and snap! Fish du jour!

MONSTERS

◀ MONSTER OR MYTH?

Sea monster sightings have been reported all over the world. The most famous of these creatures is Scotland's 'Nessie', the so-called Loch Ness Monster. Descriptions of Nessie – and a photo that turned out to be a fake – made it sound like a plesiosaur. Few people believe there are any such monsters today...but never say never!

DOWN IN THE DEPTHS ▶

With their skinny necks and roly-poly bodies, *Plesiosaurs* (PLE-see-oh-sores) may have looked awkward, but thanks to paddle-like flippers that let them twist and turn, they were able to swim at high speeds to catch food with their sharp teeth. To help themselves sink, they sometimes swallowed rocks to act as ballast. Now there's an appetizer that would fill anyone up!

FearSOME FLi

In prehistoric times, reptiles not only ruled the Earth and seas but also filled the skies. The Pterosaurs (TEH-ruh-sores), flying reptiles with wings made of skin, fed on creatures from both land and sea. Some were as tiny as a sparrow, but others had a wingspan the size of a small aeroplane's — along with knife-sharp teeth. Look out below!

▼ SUPER SCOOPER

Pteranodon (Ter-RAN-oh-don) was one funny-looking fisherman. Its head had a pointy crest and even pointier jaws. Pteranodon would skim through the water, scoop up fish and swallow them whole – the same handy method used by pelicans today.

Quetzalcoatlus (kwet-zal-co-AT-lus) was the largest creature ever to sail the skies. And sail or glide on air currents is what it probably did; its enormous wings may have been too big to flap!

ERS

AIR-VOLUTION ▶

Rhamphorynchus (RAM-foh-RING-khus), one of the early pterosaurs, had spiky teeth, great for spearing fish. It also had a long, kite-like tail that may have helped it steer through the skies. Later flying reptiles like Quetzalcoatlus looked quite different, with much shorter tails but longer necks.

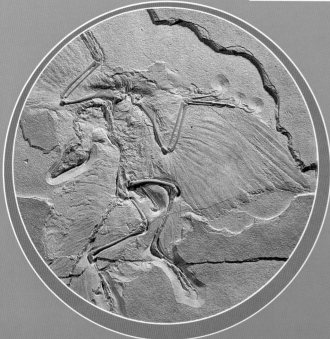

◀ FINALLY...FEATHERS!

Archeopteryx (ark-ee-OP-ter-iks), which means 'ancient wing', is the first flying reptile known to have had feathery wings. But don't let the feathers fool you – this was no ordinary bird. Its fossils reveal a skeleton of a reptile with dinosaur-like teeth and claws on its wings, which it may have used to climb trees. Some scientists think it may have been more of a glider than a flier – okay at catching a breeze, but lousy at take-offs!

The Dinos Dis

The dinosaurs (and their airborne and seafaring relatives) ruled for 165 million years. But 65 million years ago, they all disappeared. What happened? Did something kill them all at once, or did they gradually become extinct over a year...a decade...a millennium? Did one catastrophic event wipe out prehistoric life, or did a combination of factors cause this disappearing act?

VIOLENT VOLCANOES

One theory blames the dinosaurs' disappearance on huge volcanoes in what is now India. These volcanoes erupted late in the Cretaceous Period, and may have spewed so much lava, volcanic ash and poisonous gas into the air that the dinosaurs couldn't survive the climate change. Just another example of the dangers of passive smoking.

appear

LIGHTS OUT ▶

At the end of the Cretaceous Period, a massive meteorite – more than 10 kilometres wide – may have crashed down on Earth. Many scientists think that the huge clouds of dust from this collision blocked out the sun for weeks or maybe even months. Plenty of small animals (such as mammals, birds and insects) survived this big bang. However, without sunlight most plant life died. The dinosaurs would have starved to death or frozen in the freezing conditions caused by there being no sun.

BABY, IT'S COLD OUTSIDE

A less dramatic explanation of extinction is that Earth's climate changed gradually and the creatures that lived there changed with it. Once warm and tropical, our planet's weather got drier and cooler, which was fine for some creatures but devastating for dinosaurs, who couldn't handle the big chill.

Here are some of the wackier theories about what happened to the dinosaurs:

● They ate all the plants and starved to death

● Rat-sized mammals ate all their eggs

● Space aliens carried them away

What do you think?

Snakes

Snakes Alive

Snakes are part of the reptile family, but they are much more than legless lizards. Snakes can swim, they know who's about just by sticking their tongues out, and they can even fly. Love them or hate them, you'll find that they're not nearly as horrific as their reputation might suggest.

▼ EGG LAYING AND LIVE YOUNG

Most snakes lay eggs. Unlike hens' eggs, snakes' eggs feel leathery and are not hard. The majority of snakes make terrible parents, leaving eggs somewhere warm – like in rotting vegetation – and letting them get on with it. Other snakes, such as rattlesnakes, actually give birth to live young. This doesn't seem to affect the poor relationship between mother and children, though. After a just few days with mum, the young snakes face the world alone.

BLOWING HOT AND COLD ▶

In common with other reptiles, snakes cannot generate their own body heat in the way we do. Instead they use the warmth of their surroundings to get themselves moving. Sometimes they can even be spotted warming up in the early morning sun. When the temperature drops, so does their activity. And if it gets really cold it can be lethal for snakes.

Snakes have scaly bodies but, unlike fish, these are actually dry and not slimy at all.

WHERE THEY ARE FOUND

As snakes are so dependent on temperature, this factor has a big bearing on where they can live. Generally, snakes are found in the warmer parts of the world. Places like polar regions or the tops of mountains are just too cold. But snakes can and do live in water, including the world's oceans.

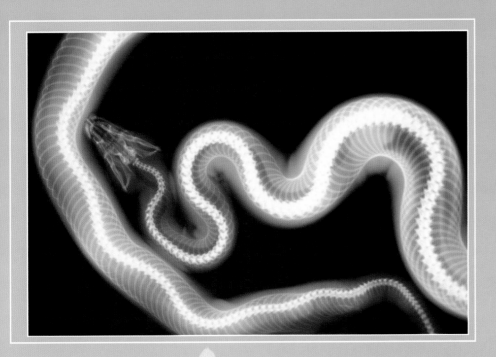

◀ BONY

Snakes get their shape from their weirdly stretched skeleton. Unlike most animals, snakes can have literally hundreds of ribs running down a backbone that reaches practically the full length of their body. What's more, on some varieties of snake, such as the python, it's possible to see a couple of little stubs of bone – the remains of legs which disappeared thousands of years ago.

Senses

Being predators, snakes have to catch other animals to live. This means their senses have to help them spot their prey before their lunch spots them. And snakes have some pretty spectacular ways of making sure that's the case.

SIXTH SENSE ▼

Most animals have a maximum of five senses – sight, hearing, touch, taste and smell – but some snakess have a sixth sense: heat. Pit vipers get their name from the small pits on the front of their faces which can detect very small changes in temperature. This is really helpful when hunting warm-blooded prey, such as mice or rats, as the prey's body heat alters the temperature of the air around them, making it easier for pit vipers to pinpoint their position.

Snakes don't just use their nostrils to smell with – they also use their tongues! If you watch a snake for any length of time you'll notice that its tongue is always popping in and out of its mouth. This isn't bad manners, it's because the snake is 'tasting' the air. It's bringing air into its mouth, where a cavity called the Jacob's organ is used to detect what is in the air particles.

▼ EAR EAR

Snakes don't have ears, so their sense of hearing is terrible. To compensate, they are good at picking up vibrations through the ground. This lets them know if something is moving around close by.

PEEK-A-BOO! ▶

Most snakes have a fairly decent sense of sight, but some types of snake can see better than others. In fact, the coachwhip snake's sense of sight is so good that it uses sight over its other senses when hunting. The trouble with snakes is that they are low to the ground and can't see far into the distance. To get around this, the snake lifts its body up into the air to peer above tall vegetation, like a periscope above the sea.

Getting About

You would think that not having any legs or arms would be a real problem when trying to get about — but not for a snake! Their long backbones and all those ribs make them very flexible, and these ingenious reptiles have devised a number of different ways of getting from A to B...

Sea snakes have adapted to life in the water so well that they are practically helpless on land.

▼ SOMETHING FISHY

The last thing you expect to see underwater are snakes, but there are a few varieties that really love the water – so much so that they spend all their lives there. Some of them, such as the Hardwicke's sea snake, have flattened tails to help push them along as they swim.

IS IT A BIRD? ▶

Why bother to climb down one tree just to climb up another one, when you can fly between them instead? The golden flying snake of southern Asia does just that though, in truth, it's really gliding. It launches itself from the top of one tree and flattens out its body in mid-air. This slows down its fall and allows it to steer itself to the neighbouring tree.

DEADLY MUSIC

The most common way for snakes to get about is by slithering along the ground. They do this by pushing against any lumps and bumps on the floor with their belly muscles. Another method, used for sneaking up on prey, is for the snake to stretch out its body then pull the rear end back up to the front – just like a concertina, but a bit more dangerous.

▲ SIDEWINDER

Snakes have adapted to move in different ways depending on the type of surface they are moving over. The sidewinder snake from the American southwest gets its name from the curious, sideways slither it has. Gripping soft, sliding sand is difficult, so sidewinders, like some other desert snakes, literally throw their bodies forwards instead of the usual snakey slither.

Bad Manners

Biting and spitting is unpleasant behaviour, but snakes don't really have time for social niceties. So be warned, these reptiles can be prickly customers.

▼ POISON

Snake poison, or 'venom' as it's called, is amazing stuff. It's made up of lots of different toxins that do different jobs. Some toxins can affect the heart or the muscles of the animal being bitten. Another toxin can break down body tissue, and yet another can cause internal bleeding. Poisonous snakes don't possess all these toxins, and not all of them cause humans too much discomfort, but it's always worth avoiding a snake bite if at all possible.

▼ FABULOUS FANGS

Snake fangs are highly developed tools – much more so than our teeth. A snake's front fangs are usually hollow, for example. This is to allow the snake to inject its victims with poison when it bites them. But that's not the end of the fang-tastic features of snake teeth. Pit vipers can make their teeth move. Normally the viper's fangs are folded away in a special pouch in the roof of their mouth, but when it's time for action the fangs swing down from the pouches and the snake's ready for dinner.

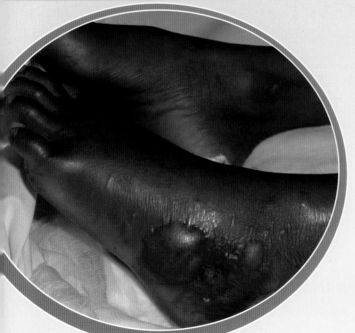

▲ SPITTING

Spitting may be a disgusting habit but it's also a great defensive move. The spitting cobra can send a stream of poisonous spit from its mouth directly into the eyes of anything it feels is a threat. The poison causes a burning sensation in the eyes and is more than enough to warn off any potential predator. Their spit is accurate up to an amazing 2.5 metres, proving you don't have to get bitten by a snake to get hurt by one.

The hognose snake has fangs at the back of its mouth for popping toads which try to inflate themselves to stop being eaten!

FRONT AND BACK ▶

Some snakes seem much friendlier than others, but you really don't want to go annoying any type of snake for the simple reason that they all have teeth. Some have big fangs at the front or back of their mouths, others have much smaller teeth, but can have up to six rows of them! Snake teeth also curve backwards, so once they've got hold of something it's unlikely their prey is going to get away.

Putting the Squeeze

Not all snakes rely on bites and poison to kill their prey. Some species of snake are known as constrictors, which means they wrap their bodies around their unfortunate victim and squeeze it to death. Constrictors don't actually crush their prey, they just squeeze it so tightly that it can't breathe and is suffocated.

TINY TERROR

Not all of the constrictors are huge giants like pythons and anacondas. Rat snakes and milk snakes also constrict their prey. Although some of these snakes get pretty big, other varieties are much less than a metre long, so they don't give larger animals much cause for concern.

THE BIGGEST OF ALL ▶

The giant of the snake world is the reticulated python. This gigantic serpent can grow over 9 metres long and is found in the Asian rainforests. Like all constrictors, pythons don't chase their prey – instead they wait in the trees to ambush their hapless victims with a lightning-quick strike, wrapping their coils around the animal before escape is possible.

▼ WATERY WONDER

Although not quite as long as the reticulated python, the real heavyweight of the snake world is the anaconda. In actual fact, anacondas are part of the boa family – the other main type of constricting snake. Anacondas are most at home in water and can be found in rivers and lakes in South America. Big enough to kill a caiman, they're the last thing you want to bump into when you're going for a swim!

Like most snakes, constrictors are more than happy to eat their prey alive if it's small enough.

► OPEN WIDE

Big snakes need big meals, so there are few animals around that needn't bother to keep a look out for these giant predators. It is certainly not unknown for pythons and anacondas to kill deer and wild pigs. But these snakes don't chew their food, so how can a python eat a deer? Easy, it unhinges its jaw and swallows the animal whole! A big meal like this can keep a snake feeling full for months.

You Have Been

Despite their reputation, snakes are not looking for trouble, in fact it's much the opposite. Generally, snakes prefer flight to fight and will go to some extraordinary lengths to warn or scare away anyone or anything which they think poses some kind of threat to them.

Snakes only bite humans as a last resort.

HOODIES ▶

One of the best tricks for scaring off a predator is to make yourself look as big as possible. Cobras are particularly good at this as they have hoods – a flap of skin behind the head which can be expanded outwards – and can raise themselves up at the same time in a truly intimidating display. Cobras are also highly poisonous, so the threat isn't just empty posturing.

Warned

SHAKE, RATTLE AND ROLL ▶

One of the most famous snake warning systems is the rattlesnake's rattle. The end of a rattlesnake's tail is made up of sections of loosely linked bony material. When a rattlesnake is threatened, it shakes this bony rattle which produces a buzzy kind of sound. As these snakes are poisonous, if you hear a rattle it's definitely worth taking heed of the warning and moving yourself away from the area as quickly as possible.

◀ BEAUTIFUL, BUT DEADLY

In common with many species of animal, snakes use colour as a warning device. Generally, a snake's colourful appearance – like this coral snake – is a warning to likely predators that the snake in question is poisonous. However, this doesn't mean that all colourful snakes are poisonous. Some non-poisonous snakes look like poisonous ones in order to fool predators into thinking they are bad news.

A VERY NASTY NOISE ▶

As we've seen with rattlesnakes, noise can be an effective way for a snake to let you know it's there and that it's not happy. They don't need a rattle to do this of course – a well directed hiss can be just as effective. The bullsnake is a master of the threatening hiss. When disturbed it can make a particular loud hiss mixed with a kind of snorty grunt that sounds particularly alarming.

Man Bites Snake

There are hundreds of different types of snake, from tiny blind snakes to giant pythons. The biggest snakes are at the top of the food chain and have no natural predator — except humans. Unfortunately, our species is proving to be a major threat to these fabulous creatures.

Getting venom from a snake is called 'milking'.

▼ BAD MEDICINE

Modern medicines extract snake venom in a very humane way, which doesn't harm the snake. Their teeth are pressed against a jar which causes the poison to seep out. Unfortunately, the same can't be said for traditional medicines, particularly in Asia, which often use chopped up snakes as part of their ingredients.

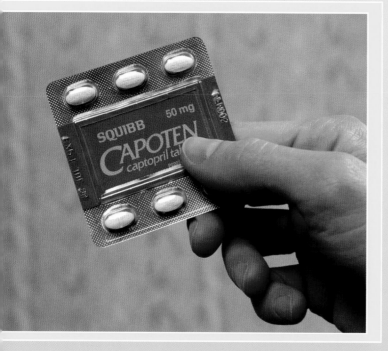

◀ KILL OR CURE

Believe it or not, snake venom could possibly save your life. It has been used to treat illnesses for hundreds of years – generally with no beneficial effects at all. Recently though, scientists have realized that there may have been something in this unorthodox treatment after all. Snake venom is now being used to create medicines which fight a whole range of illnesses including strokes, heart problems and even cancer.

BAD PUBLICITY

Most people are scared of snakes, usually for no good reason. We know that some are poisonous enough or big enough to kill us and immediately presume snakes are out to get us. In reality, snakes are very shy, but that doesn't stop people using the bad publicity they attract as an excuse for hunting them.

▼ SAVE OUR SKIN

Unfortunately for the snakes, their skin is seen as a desirable material by some clothing manufacturers. It's possible to buy snakeskin bags, belts and shoes. You can even buy jewellery made from bits of snake.

Jungle

What Is a Jungle?

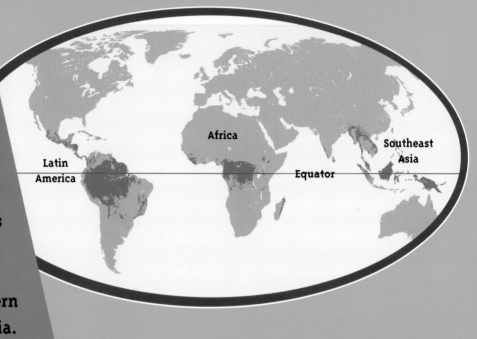

When people say jungle, they usually mean tropical rainforest. Rainforests are found around the equator — the imaginary line that circles the middle of the earth. There are rainforests in Africa, Central and Southern America, Asia and Australia.

◀ SAME BUT DIFFERENT

There are different types of tropical rainforest. The majority of the rainforest is called lowland forest, where it is warm all year round and it rains practically every day. On higher land, forests are often surrounded by clouds, hence their name of cloud forests. There are also monsoon or moist forests. These are further away from the equator where the rain does not fall in an even pattern throughout the year.

WET, WET, WET

The name is a giveaway really, but if you don't like getting wet, the rainforest is not the place for you. The weather in the lowland rainforests is very humid. There's always moisture in the air – either falling from the sky or rising as evaporation. These are ideal conditions for many plants to grow in – and they grow quickly. Each plant fights for its slice of sunlight rising higher and higher towards the sky. As a result the forest floor is a pretty dark place to be.

◀ CROWDED HOUSE

Rainforests cover only about 6 percent of the earth's surface, but it's believed they are home to around 50 percent of the world's plants and animals. In just one hectare of land it's possible to spot hundreds of different species of tree, and thousands of birds, animals and insects.

FROM THE GROUND UP

The rainforest is generally split into four levels, each with its own species of plants and animals. Starting at the bottom is, fairly obviously, the forest floor – the largest of the forest animals are found here. Next is the understory, which is the term for the smaller plants and young trees. Continue upwards and you come to the canopy, which means amongst the branches to you and me. Finally you get to the emergents – they're the show-offs of the tree world which grow taller than everyone else. They get more sunlight than the other trees, but are usually the first to fall down in high winds, too. Serves them right!

As jungles are such difficult places to explore we know that many of the plants and animals there are yet to be discovered. New species are being discovered all the time.

The Central & South

Although the Central American rainforest is one of the smaller tropical forests, the South American Amazon rainforest is the world's largest. Together they have the biggest range of animals found anywhere on earth.

Sloths spend so much of their time resting that algae grows on their fur!

▼ EAGLE-EYED PREDATOR

You may think that being able to climb to the tops of the trees would keep you safe from predators, but that's not the case here. The fearsome harpy eagle – one of the world's largest eagles – swoops over the tree tops of central and South America. It's powerful enough to hunt animals as large as monkeys.

American Jungle

◀ THE BEAR FACTS

The popular children's book character of Paddington Bear was based on South America's spectacled bear. As you might imagine, these shy creatures don't share Paddington's fondness for marmalade sandwiches. In reality, South America's only type of bear eats fruit, nuts, plants and some small animals.

A RIVER RUNS THROUGH IT

The Amazon rainforest gets its name from the mighty Amazon River which flows for nearly 6,300 kilometres from the Andes Mountains down through the jungle to the Atlantic ocean. It may not be the world's longest (it gets beaten by the Nile) but it carries more water than any other river. It's also home to thousands of species of animals including river dolphins, turtles, anacondas and the ferocious piranha fish.

TOXIC ▶

You don't have to be big to be dangerous, and with the poison dart frog the clue to their deadly nature is in the name. The frog can make poison ooze from its skin and it's deadly enough to kill a monkey-sized animal. Amerindians use the poison to tip their blow pipe darts for hunting. There are over 70 species of poison dart frog, though a few of them aren't actually poisonous. The general rule is if they're colourful, they're toxic!

The African Jungle

M ost of the African rainforest is found in the area known as central Africa. It is the second largest area of rainforest after the Amazon, and spreads over a number of different countries.

▲ JUNGLE ARMY

Even large animals have reason to fear one of the smallest predators in the jungle. Driver ants move in great swarms numbering up to millions of individuals. They have a ferocious bite, and there have been reports of driver ants eating goats, cows and even elephants!

◄ GENTLE GIANT

One animal that has suffered from a poor reputation in the past is the gorilla. Often thought to be violent creatures, these close relatives of humans are actually quite gentle and intelligent. They live in groups called troops led by the dominant male known as a silverback due to – yes, you guessed it – the grey hairs on his back.

WHO'S A PRETTY BOY THEN? ▶

Although not as vibrantly pretty as some of the macaws found in rainforests around the world, the grey parrot is one of the most talkative parrots in the world. Unfortunately, its ability to mimic sounds has also led to it becoming one of the forest's many endangered animals. Trade in these intelligent birds has been illegal for many years, but poaching still goes on.

Believe it or not, gorillas actually sleep in nests, either on the ground or in trees. They build a new one every night.

TASTY ▼

Like all rainforests, the African jungle is home to thousands of fruits and edible plants. Coffee, yams, bananas, plantains and palm oil are just a few of the foodstuffs that are valuable to people living in Africa.

LITTLE AND LARGE

You'd think that spotting an animal as big as an elephant wouldn't be so tricky – never mind a whole herd of them – but the African rainforest is so dense that it has made studying forest elephants very problematic. It's only fairly recently that scientists realised they were actually a completely different species to their larger elephant cousins which live on the African savannah.

The Asian Jungle

The rainforests of Asia cover a wide area stretching from India to Indonesia and down through New Guinea. This wide-ranging area is home to a huge variety of plants and animals.

▼ OLD MAN

If you're in Indonesia and you're really lucky you might spot an old man – but we're not talking about pensioners here. The orang-utan is often referred to as the old man of the forest. This retiring and intelligent ape is one of mankind's closest relatives, but it rarely comes down to the ground so it's difficult to see. Instead, it's happiest swinging through the trees with its long, powerful arms.

A BIG STINKER! ▶

The jungles of Borneo are home to the world's largest flower. It's called the rafflesia and its flower can grow up to one metre across. But before you head off to the garden centre to try and buy one there is a major problem with this particular plant. Its size is matched by its smell – basically, it stinks of rotting meat. Not the sort of thing you want in your garden really!

▼ PASSENGERS

Plants like rafflesia are parasites – they feed off other plants. But in the Asian jungles there is another type of plant which grows on trees but isn't parasitic. They're called epiphytes and, like this bird's nest fern, they just use the trees to hitch a lift up to where the light is better.

▲ SPOT THE PREDATOR

Many jungle animals use camouflage to hide in the shadows – this is as true of insects as it is of big predators such as leopards and tigers. The cloud leopard's markings match the dappled light and shade of the jungle perfectly.

The Asian rainforests are home to the reticulated python – the longest species of snake in the world.

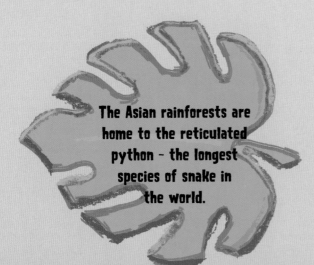

Australian Jungle

A lthough the Australian rainforest is small compared with others found across the world, it doesn't mean that it's not spectacular. Australia's remoteness from other large landmasses has allowed its wildlife to evolve in unique and surprising ways.

▲ NIGHT CRAWLER

One creature found only in the Australian rainforest is the green ringtail possum which, like the tree kangaroo, spends the vast majority of its time above ground. Like many rainforest animals, it is nocturnal, which means it is active at night. The advantage of a nocturnal lifestyle is that there are fewer predators about when it's dark. During the day, the possum sleeps on a branch curled up in a tight ball.

◄ HOPPING ALONG

The last place you'd expect to see a kangaroo is in a tree, but that's exactly where you can spot them in this rainforest. There are eleven species of tree kangaroo in the world and some are so well adapted to their life in the branches they can barely hop on the ground any more.

◀ FEELING BLUE

Rainforests are home to numerous insects, and some of the most colourful are the butterflies. One of the stars of the Australian jungle is the Ulysses butterfly, or the mountain blue as it is known. Being such a vivid blue colour – and measuring about 14 centimetres across – it's one of the easier animals to spot in the rainforest.

BEWARE OF THE PLANT

Of course, it's not just animals that can be a danger in the rainforest – sometimes the plants can cause pain and injury, too! The aptly named stinging tree produces leaves and stems which are covered in short hairs which, if touched, can stick into a person's body. What's more, the hairs are poisonous too, so on top of the cut you get an irritation which can last for months!

Tree kangaroos and possums are both marsupials, which means they carry their young babies in pouches on their fronts.

Jungle People

The rainforests are not just home to a dazzling array of plants and animals. Around 50 million people around the world call the jungle their home. Grouped into roughly 1,000 different tribes, these peoples have learnt how to live and adapt to such a difficult environment.

▲ ON THE MOVE

Can you imagine having no permanent place to call home? Many rainforest people, like this member of the Huli tribe from Papua New Guinea, are hunter-gatherers. They get their food by hunting for animals or collecting edible plants. These tribes move around a lot as they have to live where food can be found.

▶ EXTREME FARMING

When tribes like the Yanomamo of Brazil do a bit of weeding, they don't use secateurs or hoes. Instead, they employ the slash-and-burn method – chopping down trees and burning the understory. The cleared ground is then planted with fruits and edible plants. After a year or two these fields are abandoned to be reseeded by the jungle.

Indigenous people are those who belong to a certain area and have usually lived there for many centuries.

▲ FOUND IN THE FOREST

If you know what to look for, the rainforest provides food, building materials, clothes and tools – and it's all free! This house, being built by a Mbuti woman from Zaire, is made from branches and leaves – a simple structure ideally suited to the Mbuti tribe's nomadic lifestyle.

▼ PROTESTING

The rights of the forest peoples have often been ignored. Industry and logging have taken over large areas of the forests they called home. Now some Amazon rainforest tribes are fighting back. Their high-profile protests, which have gained the support of pop-stars, have secured the future of part of the forests for these tribes.

DEADLY MEETING

For many tribes, their first meeting with people from Europe was a deadly one. The European explorers brought with them diseases such as measles and small pox – illnesses which the rainforest people had never encountered before and had no natural resistance to. Tragically, whole tribes were wiped out through contact with Europeans.

SHARKS

Masters of

Shark. The very name can strike terror into many people's hearts. But sharks deserve much more than our fear — they also deserve our admiration and respect. These mysterious predators of the deep have been swimming in the world's oceans for over 450 million years — that's 200 million years before the dinosaurs! There are more than 375 different shark species, and more are still being discovered.

▼ BONELESS FISH

Unlike most fish, whose skeletons are made of bone, sharks' skeletons are made of a tough, bendable material called cartilage – the same elastic material inside our ears and noses. Cartilage is flexible and lightweight, so sharks can swim, twist and turn quickly when chasing prey.

THE DEEP

Our word 'shark' comes from the German word *Schurke*, which means 'greedy parasite' or 'scoundrel'. Sailors first used the word to describe people who had swindled them.

▲ COUSIN RAY

Although there may seem to be little family resemblance, the shark's closest relatives are rays, skates and chimeras. Like their shark cousins, they also have skeletons of cartilage. Together they make up the class *Chondrichthyes* (Con-DRIK-thees).

Most fish have an air sac called a swim bladder that helps keep them afloat, or buoyant, but sharks do not. Instead, their livers are full of oil, which is lighter than water, which helps them float. Even with their livers, sharks are still heavier than water and must keep swimming to stay buoyant.

▲ THAT'S ROUGH

Not only are sharks' mouths full of teeth, their skin is, too! A shark's body is covered in tiny, tooth-like scales called denticles. If you rub a shark's skin one way it feels smooth, but if you rub it the opposite way it is rough like sandpaper.

◄ EYE GUARD

When gripping on to thrashing, struggling prey, a shark can get poked in the eye. To protect themselves, some shark species have a special eyelid called a nictitating membrane that covers the eye just before attack. Other sharks, like the great white, roll their eyes back into their heads.

► SWIFT SWIMMERS

Even the shape of a shark's body helps make it a champion predator. Almost all sharks have a curved and tapered torpedo-shaped body, which allows it to glide smoothly – and swiftly – though the water after its prey.

Sharks are the deadliest, most successful predators in the ocean. When they hunt, all of their senses go to work, and they are just about unstoppable. They can pick up the scent of prey in the water and tracks it to its source. Sharks also uses a special sense of touch. Sensors called 'lateral lines' run the length of their bodies and help them sense movement and vibrations in the water. So sharks can 'feel' something without even touching it.

SIXTH SENSE ►

Sharks may not be able to detect ghosts, but they do have a sixth sense. Tiny pores in a shark's snout called ampullae of Lorenzini can pick up the electrical pulses that all living things give off. This 'electro-sense' helps the shark pinpoint the exact location of its prey so it can strike with amazing accuracy.

FIND YOU WITH!

Some sharks can smell a single drop of blood in the water half a kilometre away.

Some sharks travel hundreds of kilometres every year to breeding and feeding grounds and never get lost. How do they find their way? Scientists aren't sure, but they think sharks may use their 'electro-sense' like a compass, to detect changes in the Earth's magnetic field.

Better to eat

The dinner menu is quite similar for most kinds of sharks. They prefer smaller fish (including other sharks) and invertebrates such as squid. Bottom-dwelling sharks, like the wobbegong, however, eat shrimps, crabs and other crustaceans that live near the ocean floor. Large sharks, like the great white and the bull shark, also feed on marine mammals. Unlike most sharks, tiger sharks are notoriously unfussy about what they eat — they will swallow just about anything they can get their massive jaws on.

▲ DENTAL CARE

Every time a shark eats, some of its teeth either break or fall out. Luckily, every time a tooth falls out, a replacement tooth from the row behind is waiting to take its place. Some sharks have ten or more rows of teeth and can go through over 20,000 teeth in a lifetime!

◄ TAKE A BITE

One of the weirdest feeders of all is the cookie-cutter shark. Its round mouth is specially designed to take cookie-sized bites out of larger animals like whales and dolphins. It is about as long as a skateboard, and its 'cookie bites' are not fatal.

YOU   with!

▶ Filter Feeders

The largest sharks in the ocean – the whale shark, megamouth, and basking shark – eat some of the ocean's smallest food: microscopic plants and animals called plankton. Their mouths act like giant strainers to filter tiny plankton out of the water. The 10 metre-long basking shark (right) filters 1,485,000 litres of water an hour – enough to fill a large swimming pool.

Some of the more items found in a tiger shark's stomach include car registration plates, shoes, weights, tin cans and an alarm clock.

A shark's jaws are not connected to its skull, so it can move both its top and bottom jaws out and forward, allowing it to open its mouth really wide. The shark then snaps its powerful jaws shut, just like a trap.

The good, the bad

The 375 known shark species come in a variety of sizes and shapes, each one specially adapted to its particular lifestyle. The biggest, the whale shark, can grow more than 15 metres long, while the smallest, the pygmy shark, is less than 15 centimetres long and can fit in the palm of your hand. Sharks can be spotted or striped, flat-bodied or round — some deep water sharks even glow in the dark!

▼ FUNNY FACE

Hammerhead sharks, with their strange, T-shaped heads, are easy to recognize. Their eyes, which are on either side of their broad, flat heads, give them excellent all-around vision. These sharks use their heads to pin prey, such as stingrays, to the ocean floor.

The fastest shark is the shortfin mako, which can swim up to 48 kilometres per hour in short bursts.

▶ SPOT THE SHARK

Many bottom-dwelling sharks, like this tasselled wobbegong, are covered in spots, blotches or stripes so that they blend in with plants and rocks on the sea floor. This helps them hide from enemies and also catch unsuspecting prey.

and the ugly

HORNSHARK ▲

The hornshark gets its name from the two sharp spines that stick out from its dorsal fins. The spines make predators think twice before attacking. This 1-metre-long shark lives on the ocean floor off the coast of California and Mexico.

▶ MAKE YOUR MIND UP: SPOTS OR STRIPES?

Baby zebra sharks have black and yellow stripes, but as the sharks grow, the markings change into pale brown spots. The adults are therefore sometimes called leopard sharks.

Many sharks are dark on top and pale underneath. When seen from above, they blend in with the dark waters below, and from underneath they match the sunlit waters above.

The heavyweights

Introducing, in this corner, the most infamous shark to swim the ocean, the most feared predator in the sea — the great white. In the far corner, the largest shark in the world, also known as the 'gentle giant' — the whale shark. How do these two heavyweights of the shark world measure up?

▲ JAWS - THE TRUTH EXPOSED!

In 1975, the movie *Jaws* made many people afraid to go into the water. But the great white shark in that movie could never have existed in real life; the film makers built a mechanical shark with extra teeth and wrong-size fins; it would sink if it were real. When real sharks were filmed, small, model divers made them look bigger than they were.

GREAT WHITE

Scientific name:
Carcharodon carcharias

Size: Also known as the 'white death' or the 'white pointer', the great white is the largest flesh-eating shark. It is about 6 metres long and weighs over 2 tonnes.

Colouring: It has a very distinctive two-tone colouring. Its upper body is blue to grey, while its underbelly is much lighter, even white.

Range: The great white shark lives in cool waters in subtropical and temperate seas.

Diet: With its 5-cm-long serrated teeth, the great white eats fish and sea mammals like seals and sea lions.

Scientists now believe that many of the attacks blamed on the great white are actually committed by the bull shark.

▲ WHALE SHARK

Scientific Name: *Rhincodon typus*

Size: It is named after its size. Measuring over 14 metres long and weighing more than 13 tonnes, the whale shark is the largest shark, and the largest fish, in the world.

Colouring: On top it is blue-grey, but underneath it is white. Its skin is camouflaged with distinctive white spots and bars to help it blend in with the surrounding water.

Range: The whale shark lives in warm waters on either side of the equator, both in the open ocean and near the shore.

Diet: Plankton. The shark flushes huge mouthfuls of water over its gill rakers (walls of spongy mesh inside its throat). The gill rakers act as a sieve, trapping the plankton for the shark to swallow.

▲ BIG MOUTH, TINY TEETH

The whale shark's mouth is lined with thousands of tiny teeth, each one about the size of a grain of rice.

HUMAN-INFESTED

Despite the frightening attacks you may have seen in films, shark attacks on humans are extremely rare. There are about 50 attacks reported each year, out of which only two or three are fatal. In fact, humans have more to fear from mosquitoes than from sharks. Bites from malaria-carrying mosquitoes kill 2 to 3 million people every year, making mosquitoes a million times more lethal than sharks. There are four 'usual suspects' in most shark attacks on humans. They are the tiger, bull, great white and oceanic whitetip shark.

More people are injured by coconuts falling on their heads than are injured by sharks!

▼ MY MISTAKE

Many shark attacks on humans are a case of mistaken identity. To a shark, a diver wearing a wet suit and flippers, or a surfer on a surfboard, can look like its favourite food – a seal or a sea turtle.

WATERS

▲ POLLUTION

Sharks are also threatened by pollution. Chemicals in the water kill the fish they eat, while oil spills destroy important breeding grounds. Sharks mature very slowly and give birth to few young. Often sharks are killed, either by overfishing or pollution, more quickly than they can reproduce.

▲ HUMAN ATTACK!

The truth is, we are far more dangerous to sharks than they are to us. Every year, 100 million sharks are killed by humans – that's 275,000 sharks a day! They are fished for their meat, skin, teeth, oil and just for fun. Many sharks are accidentally caught in nets meant for other fish.

▼ SOUVENIR HUNTERS

Sharks are killed for their jaws as well, which are removed and sold as souvenirs. If you are tempted to buy one, remember where it came from.

Chances are a shark will never attack you, but here are some ways to avoid close encounters of the shark kind:

● Don't swim where sharks have been seen.

● Don't swim alone. Sharks will attack a lone swimmer before threatening a group.

● If you see a shark, swim calmly to the boat or shore. Splashing and panicking will only attract a shark.

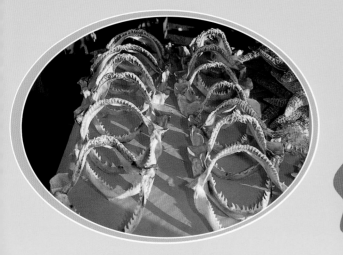

S.O.S.—Save Our

So many sharks are killed each year that several kinds, including the great white, blue and basking shark, are in big trouble. They are classified as threatened species, meaning their numbers are dwindling so rapidly that conservationists warn they could soon be in danger of dying out altogether. If shark species died out, all of ocean life would suffer. As top-of-the-food-chain predators, sharks keep many fish populations in check; as scavengers, sharks help keep the oceans clean.

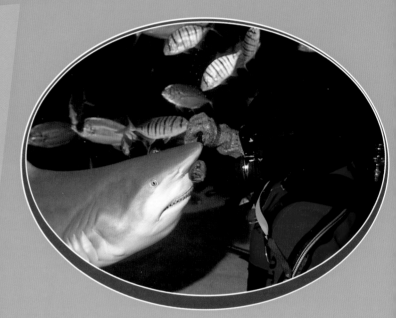

◀ HEALTH SHARKS

Sharks don't lose many days to sickness because they don't often get diseases. Finding out why sharks are so healthy could one day help us discover how to avoid serious diseases like cancer.

SPIRITS OF THE DEEP ▶

Sharks are important symbols for native peoples around the world. In Hawaii, people believed that the shark god Kamohoali would help lost fishermen by leading their canoes through fog and mist. Some Pacific Islanders believe sharks are the spirits of their dead ancestors.

Sharks

Aquariums also play a part in helping sharks. By allowing visitors to get a close-up view of live sharks, they help us understand that sharks are worth far more alive than dead.

◄ WHAT IS BEING DONE?

Many marine biologists and conservation groups are working very hard to make sure we don't hunt our sharks to extinction. Biologists study sharks in their natural environment to learn more about their behaviour and life history. The more we know about sharks, the more we can do to help save them. Conservation groups spread the word about sharks in danger, pressure governments to pass laws protecting sharks, and set up underwater nature reserves where sharks can live without danger of being fished by humans.

We must help change the shark's reputation as a ruthless man-eater so it will be respected and preserved.

T. REX

KiNg OF tHe

As we know from earlier in this book, huge, magnificent reptiles ruled the earth for around 160 million years before disappearing in mysterious circumstances about 65 million years ago. Dinosaurs came in all shapes and sizes, from the huge, long-necked *Brachiosaurus* (brak-ee-oh-SORE-us), taller than six adults, to the scurrying chicken-sized *Compsognathus* (comps-sog-NAYTH-us). However, one stands out from all the rest, the world's most famous dinosaur species, *Tyrannosaurus rex* (tie-RAN-o-SORE-us rex). But what was this dinosaur really like? Was it as fearsome as it first appears? What did it eat? How fast could it run? What colour was it? These are all questions which people are still trying to answer today.

▲ BIG BOY

Tyrannosaurus rex was the largest of the Tyrannosaur family of dinosaurs which lived in North America around 85 to 65 million years ago. Tyrannosaurus rex was also one of the biggest carnivorous, or meat-eating, dinosaurs ever discovered. It measured over 13 metres from nose to tail, was over 4 metres high – though if it stretched up, T. rex could have reached up to 6 metres. It weighed between 6 and 8 tonnes, too, which means it was heavier that an elephant and longer than two minibuses.

Dinosaurs

END OF AN ERA

The period of history when the dinosaurs were alive is called the Mesozoic era. The same types of dinosaurs weren't alive for all of this time, so the Mesozoic era is split into three different periods. The first two are called the Triassic and the Jurassic periods. Tyrannosaurus rex was alive at the end of the reign of the dinosaurs. This was known as the Cretaceous period.

The name Tyrannosaurus rex means 'tyrant lizard king'. It is thought that female Tyrannosaurs were bigger than males.

▶ CHANGING WORLD

The Cretaceous world was very different from the one we know today. Even the shape of the continents was different. The land was still moving about, and most of it had been in two large lumps called Gondwana and Laurasia. By the time T. rex appeared these land masses had broken up and started to form the continents we see today.

KEEP OFF THE GRASS ▶

On the land things were pretty different, too. The closest you would get to mammals like us were four-legged, furry creatures, most no bigger than a mouse. You might recognize some of the vegetation such as figs, ferns, conifers, ginkgos and sycamores, but there were no grasses. At least you didn't have to worry about T. rex ruining your lawn!

69

Fearsome Find

There have been around 30 T. rex skeletons discovered so far, and not all of these are in good condition or anywhere near complete. For these reasons, a good specimen attracts a lot of attention — as in the case of the Field Museum of Chicago's prize exhibit.

▲ FEMME FATALE

The most famous Tyrannosaurus rex of all can be found at the Field Museum in Chicago and is known as Sue. She is one of the most complete skeletons of a T. rex found so far and is also the largest. The skeleton was so well preserved it helped palaeontologists (people who study ancient life such as dinosaurs) to learn a great deal more about these magnificent dinosaurs than ever before.

SIOUX SUE OVER SUE

Sue was discovered in 1990 near Faith in South Dakota, by a team from the Black Hills Institute. Soon a huge row erupted over who actually owned the skeleton. The team that found her, the Sioux Indians on whose reservation she had been found, a man called Maurice Williams who owned the ranch where Sue was found, and the government all claimed Sue was theirs. It was a real legal mess and Sue was kept locked away for years before it was sorted out. In the end, it was decided the rancher owned it and Sue was auctioned in 1997. She was bought for $8.4 million by the Field Museum in Chicago.

▲ NUMBER ONE

The first Tyrannosaurus rex found was discovered by a fossil hunter called Barnum Brown in 1902. Today, scientists like Jack Horner are continuing his work.

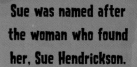
Sue was named after the woman who found her, Sue Hendrickson.

STAN THE MAN ▲

Although the Black Hill's Institute doesn't have Sue, they do have another famous T. rex called Stan. This skeleton was found in Hell's Creek, South Dakota by an amateur fossil hunter called Stan Sacrison. Like Sue, Stan had suffered some injuries in its life, such as broken bones – probably from fights with other Tyrannosaurs!

MOVING MONSTER ▶

Improvements in robotic engineering mean that moving, or animatronic, models are all the rage now. Visitors to museums such as London's Natural History Museum can get within touching distance of a ferocious roaring Tyrannosaur – luckily this is as close as we'll ever get to being face to face with a T. rex.

Straight to

Without a doubt, it's the Tyrannosaur's fearsome head that makes it such a scary and impressive dinosaur. At around 1.5 metres long, its skull was as big as your average 12 year-old kid and was packed full of dangerous looking teeth. This was the business end of the T. rex, and other dinosaurs were well-advised to keep clear of it.

Tyrannosaurs were always growing new teeth, so when an old one fell or got knocked out, a new one was ready to replace it.

MOUTHFUL OF MISERY

If you were unfortunate enough to see inside a Tyrannosaur's mouth, you'd see up to 60 good reasons to want to be somewhere else. Its teeth could measure up to 15 centimetres long and curved backwards, meaning unlucky prey couldn't get away in a hurry.

the POINT

MEET THE NEIGHBOURS

As big and fearsome as Tyrannosaurus rex was, unbelievably it may not have been the largest meat-eating dinosaur of the Cretaceous period. *Giganotosaurus* (gi-GAN-oto-SORE-us) from Argentina and *Carcharodontosaurus* (car-CHA-row-DON-toe-SORE-us) from Morocco might well have been bigger. However, T. rex appears to be heavier than both of these giant meat-eaters.

▼ SMALL ARMS

Another big question – what were the T. rex's arms for? They were so small they couldn't reach the Tyrannosaur's mouth, and would be useless for picking things up as they only had two claws at the end. However, these two claws were really sharp and palaeontologists have also worked out that the arms were very strong – a puzzling, if short, mystery.

▲ BIG BITE

A Tyrannosaurus rex's mouth was big enough to swallow a human whole, and it's no surprise that such a big mouth could give one heck of a big bite. Scientists have worked out that a T. rex could easily chomp its way through thick dinosaur bones. Anything unlucky enough to get in its way would be lucky to survive.

Savager or

E veryone agrees that Tyrannosaurs were the super-carnivores of their time. But what palaeontologists can't agree on is whether this fearsome looking dinosaur hunted for its food or was a scavenger. Animals which scavenge look for other animals who have died or already been killed, instead of hunting live prey. The hunter or scavenger question is the big debating point about Tyrannosaurs.

▲ HEADSTRONG

If T. rex was a scavenger why did it have such a strong head? The skull bones are really tough and could easily handle a strong impact, such as the sort you would expect if it was attacking another dinosaur.

◄ BIG NOSE

Palaeontologists who argue that T. rex was a scavenger point out that it had a very good sense of smell. Scavengers, such as vultures, can smell rotting meat from great distances. But maybe T. rex needed a good sense of smell for tracking down its prey.

Scavenger?

SLOWCOACH

One thing's for sure, Tyrannosaurus rex was no speed freak. After studying the dinosaur's leg bones and muscles, scientists believe Tyrannosaurs had a top speed of about 40 kilometres per hour – faster than a human, but pretty slow when compared to many dinosaurs. Worse still, it seems that T. rex could only keep up this speed for a short sprint. Could such a slowcoach catch other animals, or didn't it matter in dense forests?

EYE CAN SEE YOU ▶

One of the strongest arguments in favour of Tyrannosaurus being a hunter rather than a scavenger is the position of its eyes. The eyes face forwards, like a human's do, rather than to the sides, like a horse. Forward-facing eyes give a better sense of exactly where objects are, which is why top predators such as tigers have eyes in this position. Then again, so do some scavengers such as hyenas.

OVER TO YOU

Hunter or scavenger – what do you think? Perhaps T. rex did a bit of both.

DANGEROUS

W hat was life like for a baby Tyrannosaur? Certainly the Cretaceous forest was a dangerous place for a juvenile. They could be crushed by large plant-eating dinosaurs or eaten by other carnivores. There was even a possibility that the young Tyrannosaurs might get eaten by one of their parents. Life was certainly on the rough side for kids in the Cretaceous.

◀ HATCHING OUT

Like all dinosaurs, Tyrannosaurus would have started life in an egg. Some palaeontologists think that the eggs may have been long and thin, as this may have been the best shape for a T. rex. If there were eggs, then there was probably a nest. It seems unlikely that Tyrannosaurs sat on their nests, as they would surely be too heavy for the eggs. Perhaps they covered the eggs in earth or leaves, too, in much the same way that crocodiles do today to keep their eggs warm.

FEATHERED FRIEND ▶

Many people believe that birds are descended from dinosaurs. Recent finds in China back up this idea as they show that some dinosaurs had feathers. Now some palaeontologists suggest that some baby dinosaurs may have had feathers to keep them warm, too.

GROUPIES?

It's generally believed that Tyrannosaurs were solitary dinosaurs, because adult skeletons are usually found by themselves. However, nobody really knows if T. rex lived in groups or not. If they did live in a pack, it would certainly have made hunting easier for fairly slow dinosaurs like these.

Some people believe that all dinosaurs had feathers. Can you imagine T. rex as a ferocious type of chicken?

GOOD PARENTS

Were Tyrannosaurs good parents? Some palaeontologists think that a mother Tyrannosaur, like many carnivorous predators today such as lions, would have looked after her young, teaching them either how to hunt or how to find carrion (dead animals). However, some also believe that male Tyrannosaurs would see young Tyrannosaurs as a threat, and would try to kill and eat them. That doesn't sound like good parenting!

How Do We

Everything we know about dinosaurs comes from the painstaking work of fossil-hunters, palaeontologists and other scientists. We now know more than ever about dinosaurs, and the newest technology is being used to try and find out more. Fossils are scanned, magnified and x-rayed, and computers are used to try and work out what the dinosaurs looked like and how they moved and lived. But there's still plenty we don't know.

▼ GOING UNDERGROUND

Preparing fossils is a time-consuming business. Getting from the moment a fossil is discovered to the time it appears in a museum can take thousands of hours of work. For example, it took years to dig up Sue's remains and prepare her for display.

A QUESTION OF COLOUR

Fossils can tell us a great deal, but they can't tell us what colour T. rex was, so paleontologists look at animals today for clues. Hunters, such as lions, aren't bright pink in colour as they would be spotted a mile off. Instead they are a dull colour to blend into the background. Perhaps the same would be true for T. rex, too.

KNOW?

The only way palaeontologists will find out more about dinosaurs is if more fossils are found. So keep your eyes on the ground and get fossil finding!

◀ DIRTY BUSINESS

Being a palaeontologist isn't very glamorous, especially if your job is inspecting dinosaur poo to discover what dinosaurs ate. Fossilized poo is called coprolite, and it can tell palaeontologists a lot about dinosaur diets. It's a dirty job but someone's got to do it.

SOUND OF SILENCE

Fossils can't tell us what sort of noise the T. rex made either. Did it roar, or did it squeak, cluck, hiss or bark?

WARM OR COLD?

Another question puzzling palaeontologists is whether T. rex was warm or cold-blooded. Mammals like tigers, horses and we humans are warm-blooded. This means our bodies are ready to go as soon as we wake up. Reptiles are cold-blooded, which means they need to warm up in the sun before they can start moving about. Dinosaurs were reptiles so they could be cold-blooded. Birds, however, which many palaeontologists believe evolved from dinosaurs, are warm-blooded. Also, how long would it take a big dinosaur like T. rex to warm up in the morning?

REPTILES

What is a

What do you think of when you hear the words 'reptile' or 'amphibian'? Many people think of cold, slimy snakes, but they couldn't be more wrong. True, snakes are reptiles, but they are nothing like you might imagine, and they are just one member of the extended reptile clan. There are over seven thousand types of reptile and way more than four thousand kinds of amphibian all of which come in lots of shapes and sizes, from giant lizards and huge tortoises to the tiniest of frogs.

MEET THE ANCESTORS ▶

Even the biggest of today's lizards don't match up to their huge predecessors, the dinosaurs. That's right; those mighty monsters from the past were all reptiles, too. So the next time a snake gives you the shivers or a turtle gives you a fright, be thankful it isn't a T. rex instead. In fact, reptiles were around long before the dinosaurs appeared. The oldest fossil reptile found so far is over 340 million years old. And amphibians are even older – some fossils date back over 360 million years.

Reptile?

BIG AND SMALL ▼

Even though today's reptiles aren't as big as before, they still cover a wide range of sizes. Anacondas, giant South American snakes, can grow up to between 8 and 11 metres in length – that's about the length of two and a half family cars. At the other end of the scale, the smallest reptiles are geckos. Some don't grow any longer than around 2.5 centimetres.

People who study reptiles are called herpetologists.

SUN LOVERS ▶

Reptiles can be found virtually anywhere, whether it's in a high-rise in Los Angeles, a desert in Africa, or even in the depths of the Indian Ocean. But you'll not find one in most Arctic areas or in Antarctica. That's due to the fact that reptiles don't like the cold, so you'll never bump into one on a ski slope!

Body Bits

S o, what makes a reptile what it is? Although they may look very different from each other, all reptiles have some things in common — even if it doesn't seem like it at first.

▼ NOT GOOD IN THE MORNING

Reptiles are often called cold-blooded, which means they can't generate their own body heat. Instead, reptiles have to rely on the sun to warm them up. Reptiles are very sluggish when they haven't warmed up enough, which makes it easy for predators to catch them. The warmer it is, the quicker reptiles warm up, which is why reptiles don't live in cold areas.

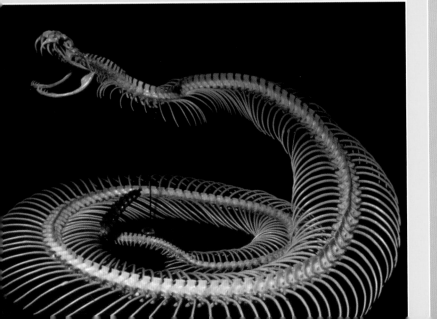

◄ BITS AND PIECES

All reptiles have a skeleton with a backbone and lay eggs, which have a waterproof shell. Remarkably, reptiles all either have four legs or had ancestors which had four legs — this also includes snakes. Of course, snakes lost their legs a long time ago, but their ancestors had them and you can still see small traces of legs on some snakes' skeletons.

SCALES ▼

All reptiles have scales, which are made from keratin – the same stuff your fingernails are made from. Their skin is also very dry as it is specially designed to stop reptiles from losing water from their bodies. On some reptiles, such as crocodiles, the scales fuse together to form plates, which makes the skin tougher.

Reptiles can virtually shut their bodies down if they get too cold.

GOING UP ▶

Reptiles are great climbers and this is due to their special feet. Reptiles have clawed feet, which are an obvious help. But some lizards, such as geckos, have millions of little hairs, called 'setae', on the bottom of their feet. These tiny hairs allow geckos to climb walls with the greatest of ease.

It's Dragon

When people first found fossils they imagined they must be the bones of monsters or dragons. Then, when explorers and traders went to foreign climates and saw some of the biggest and most fearsome-looking reptiles, they came back with even taller tales of gigantic beasts. They may not be gigantic, but these modern-day monsters are still impressive creatures.

It was once believed that a stare from a basilisk lizard was enough to kill you!

▼ WORTH MONITORING

The heavyweights of the lizard world are the monitors, and king amongst them is the Komodo dragon. Found only on the island of Komodo and some neighbouring islands, these fearsome creatures grow to over 3 metres and weigh more than two people put together. They are big enough to kill and eat deer and have even been known to eat children!

Time

▼ PROUD PARENTS

A crocodile might be the last thing you want to see when you're going for a swim, but as far as their babies are concerned, they're great parents. Crocodiles are one of the few members of the reptile family who take care of their young. They build or dig nests for their eggs and, when they hatch, the crocodile is there to take care of its new brood. Some species even carry their babies from the nest to the water edge in their mouth – and aren't tempted to eat a single one!

▲ SNEAKY SNAPPER

There are over 20 species of crocodilian, including crocodiles, alligators, and caimans. The biggest are saltwater crocodiles which can grow to over 6 metres long and weigh more than a car. Crocodilians are very good at hiding in the water – even the big ones – and ambush their prey, sneaking up on them as they drink before lunging out of the water to grab them. In fact, some species of crocodile can even jump straight up out of the water.

NOT A PRETTY SIGHT ▶

The marine iguana is so odd-looking that even the renowned naturalist Charles Darwin described them as 'disgusting'. However, he was probably impressed by their swimming skills as this strange lizard can stay underwater for up to an hour.

Snakes Alive

R ight at the top of the list of things which people are scared of are snakes. Most people with a snake phobia have never seen a snake, and it's fair to say that they get a bad rap. In reality, snakes aren't at all like you'd imagine. They're very shy animals and are much happier scurrying away from people than attacking them. Many snakes are harmless anyway, and even the most poisonous ones will only bite if provoked or surprised.

▼ FANG–TASTIC

Poisonous snakes don't have the biggest fangs you're likely to see in the animal kingdom, but they're very effective at what they do. Like hypodermic needles, snakes' fangs are perfect for injecting poison into their prey.

Some snakes, such as rattlesnakes, have movable fangs which fold back into the roof of the mouth when they're not needed.

HOODED KING ▶

Some of the world's snakes are venomous, which means they inject poison into their prey when they bite them. By far the most famous venomous snake is the cobra with its distinctive hood of skin behind its head. The largest of the cobra family is the king cobra, which is so venomous that it can kill an elephant with a single bite.

▲ BIG SQUEEZE

The biggest snakes are the constrictors – snakes like pythons and boas which crush their prey to death by wrapping them in their coils and squeezing really tightly. The largest snakes of all are anacondas, which live in rivers in South America.

▼ OPEN WIDE

Swallowing your food down whole without chewing it may sound like terrible table manners, but it's exactly what snakes do. Snakes have fangs but no teeth for chewing; instead they have very flexible jaws. When it comes to meal times, snakes open their mouths as wide as possible and swallow their prey whole – always head first, as it's easier to swallow that way.

Over 7,000 people are bitten by snakes in America every year. Luckily, very few cases prove fatal.

Hard Shell

Y ou might know them as slow-moving lettuce chompers, and it's true that often tortoises and turtles don't seem in much of a hurry, but the chelonian family includes some truly remarkable animals. Some species travel thousands of kilometres across the oceans, others can live longer than practically any other animal on earth. Take a peek under the shell of the chelonians and meet the truly terrific tortoises, turtles and terrapins.

▲ HARD CASE

All members of the chelonian family have a shell. The shell is part of the turtles' skeleton and is generally very hard and protective. Some chelonians can even bring their legs, head and tail into the shell for extra protection. But not all chelonian shells are hard. The leatherback turtle, for example, has a soft shell. This is because this turtle swims to great depths in the sea where the water pressure would otherwise crack it.

WHAT'S WHAT? ▶

All chelonians are turtles, but people tend to call different ones different names. As a general rule of thumb, a tortoise lives on land and a turtle lives in the water. In the UK, a turtle that lives in freshwater is called a terrapin.

FLIPPING BRILLIANT ▼

There are over 250 species of turtles and tortoises, and many of them spend their time in water. Only seven species of turtle spend all their time in the ocean. These sea turtles, like this loggerhead turtle, have large flippers instead of legs to help them swim, and only come on land to lay their eggs.

▲ UNDER THREAT

Like many members of the reptile and amphibian families, turtles are under threat. Loss of habitat, hunting, poaching and pollution are slowly killing off some species of these ancient, stately creatures. In some countries, it is now illegal to have a tortoise as a pet unless it has been born in the same country.

GENTLE GIANTS ▶

Some of the most famous tortoises of all are those found on the Galapagos Islands of the Pacific Ocean. These giants can measure over 1 metre from head to tail and weigh over 200 kilograms. Even more remarkably, these gentle giants can live for between 150 and 200 years.

Amphibian

When people talk about reptiles they often mean amphibians as well. In fact, amphibians are entirely different creatures, but just as amazing. The easiest way to tell them apart is to look at the skin. All reptiles have scales, but amphibians don't. Amphibian skin is much thinner than reptile skin, and amphibians also lose moisture through their skin, which is why they live in water or damp environments.

DON'T TOUCH ▲

Some amphibians aren't quick enough to escape predators, so they've come up with a clever way of protecting themselves – they poison their attackers! When threatened, the amphibians ooze poison from their skin, which not only tastes bad but could possibly kill some predators.

SURPRISE SURPRISE ▶

Even though frogs and toads prefer warm, damp conditions you'd be surprised where they turn up. They don't all live by the sides of ponds – you'll find them in trees in the rainforests of South America and even in the deserts of Australia. These desert-living frogs spend much of their time buried underground waiting for the rain to return.

Fun

FROG OR TOAD? ▼

How can you tell the difference between a frog and a toad? Look at the skin – if it's smooth it's a frog, if bumpy it's probably a toad.

▲ FOND OF FIRE?

Salamanders are secretive creatures, often confused with lizards. Many old wives tales grew up about these amphibians, the most famous one being that they could not be harmed by fire. This, of course, is absolute nonsense. Perhaps someone threw a log where a salamander was hiding onto a fire and spotted it scurrying away.

▼ NEWT NEWS

Newts are part of the salamander family. Some newts live on the land and others in the water, but like many amphibians, they all breed in water. Young newts live on land for the first 2 years and then return to the water to breed or to live permanently.

SQUIRMY WORMY ▲

Is it a snake? Is it an eel? Is it a worm? No – it's a caecilian. These blind, legless amphibians spend most of their lives underground and use their sense of smell to find their food.

You can't get warts from handling toads!

Frills and

W ith so many different types of reptile and amphibian, it should come as no surprise that some of them look a little odd. And sometimes their behaviour is just as strange, too.

▲ TREE HOPPER

You can find reptiles everywhere – under the ground, up trees, on the water, in the water and even in the air. Some tree-dwelling lizards have taken to springing into the air to reach trees that are too far away to reach. Although called flying dragons, these reptiles in fact use special flaps of skin to help them glide, like a hang-glider, from tree to tree.

▲ WALKING ON WATER

If a basilisk lizard is in a hurry and there's water in its path, the lizard won't go round it or swim across it. Instead, it picks up speed and runs over the top of it on two legs. This miraculous behaviour earned it the name the Jesus lizard.

▲ BUG EYED MARVEL

The chameleon is a remarkable beast. Not only does it have poppy-out eyes which can move in opposite directions to each other and a long tongue which can shoot out to catch flies, it can also change colour. It is often thought that chameleons change colour to blend into their background, but some scientists believe the colour change happens to show when a chameleon is angry or feels threatened.

Spills

PARENTS WITH POUCHES ▶

Some frogs and toads go to extraordinary lengths to take care of their eggs and young. The Suriname toad actually carries her eggs around on her back, where they sit embedded into her skin. Some frogs have pouches like kangaroos where their young can grow up in safety.

Some lizards' tails snap off if they're captured so they can escape.

PUTTING ON A SHOW ▶

If reptiles feel threatened, the first thing they do is try to get away. If reptiles get cornered, however, they have different ways of reacting. Some reptiles will play dead, rattlesnakes will shake the tip of their tails to produce a rattling noise as a warning, but one of the most startling of displays comes from the frilled lizard of Australia. This lizard will spread out a frill around its head and hiss at the animal chasing it. The frill makes the lizard look much bigger than it is and, hopefully, puts off the attacker.

BIG CATS

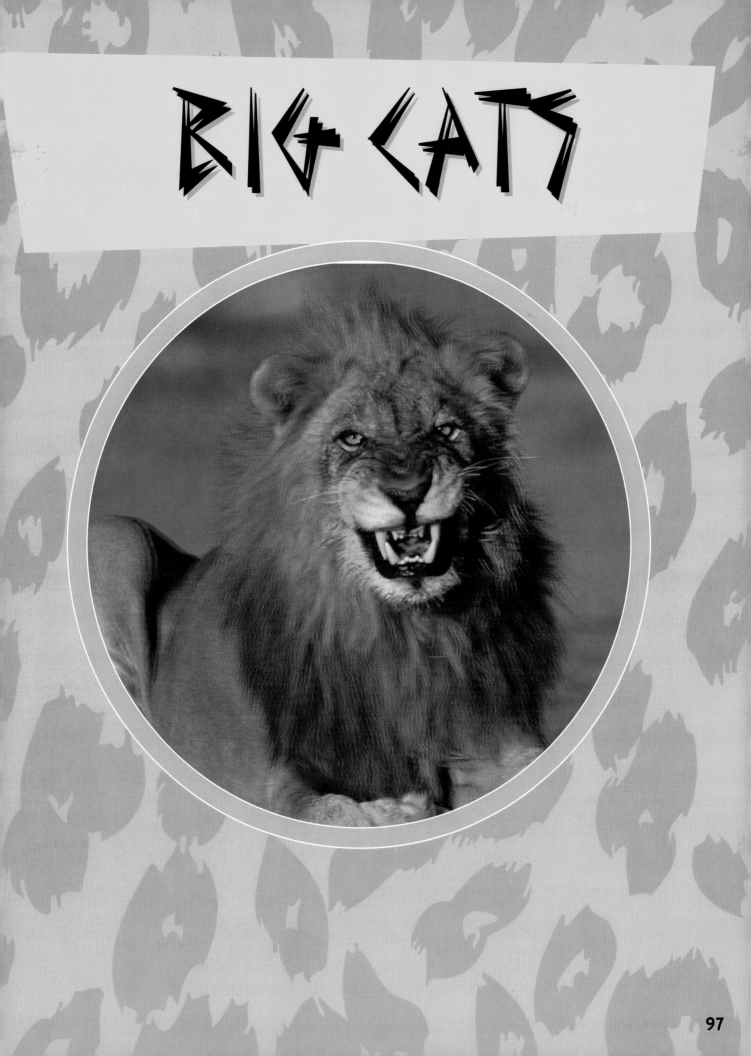

The history of the cat stretches back over 30 million years, and today there are over 30 different species. At the top of this feline pile are the big cats. Although this is a rather general group, when people talk about big cats they often mean tigers, lions, leopards, cheetahs, cougars and jaguars.

▲ WHAT BIG TEETH YOU HAVE

One of the most famous cats was the sabre-tooth, which died out about 10,000 years ago. This fearsome predator had a massive pair of pointy teeth which it used to stab its prey.

▲ SAME DIFFERENCE

All cats are basically the same, whether it's the humble tabby or the majestic lion. They all have an excellent sense of smell and sight and like to keep clean. All cats are carnivores, too, which means they are meat-eaters – and the bigger the cat, the bigger the meal they need.

Big cats are found in the wild on every continent except Antarctica, Australia and Europe.

Cats?

▲ UNDER THREAT

Despite being top predators, many species of big cat are under threat of extinction. Some cats are hunted for their skins which are used to make clothes or rugs, or are killed for their bones and teeth, which are used in some traditional medicines. Even though these cats are protected they are still hunted by poachers.

▲ NOW YOU SEE THEM

Spotty or stripy, or even a plain dusty brown colour, each type of cat's coat serves the same purpose – it helps them to hide. All big cats have to catch their food, so the longer they can stay hidden from their prey the more chance the cat has of sneaking up and catching it.

WHAT'S BEING DONE? ▶

Many organizations are trying to protect big cats. One way is to educate people as to how important big cats are to the local economy. A dead cat can bring big money for poachers, but a live cat can bring in more money from rich tourists who want to see the cats in the wild. Also, farmers don't mind losing cattle so much if they are paid for each animal that gets eaten by a cat.

Tigers

The tiger is the most recognizable of all the big cats, with its orangey-red stripy body. It is also the biggest of all big cats, with the Siberian, or Amur, tiger being the biggest species of all. These huge cats can grow up to 4 metres long and weigh as much as four people.

WHERE ARE THEY FOUND?

Tigers can be found in India, Siberia, and South-East Asia. There are five types of tiger alive today, but there used to be more spread across a much bigger area.

▲ GOOD MOTHER

Tigers are solitary creatures, like most big cats, except when a mother tiger is raising her young. Tiger cubs stay with their mothers for around 2 years until the cubs leave to find their own territories. During those years, the mother will teach her cubs how to survive in the wild. One of the most important lessons is how to stalk and hunt prey – if you don't eat, you don't survive.

◄ MAN HUNTER

Tigers are one of the few big cats who will occasionally hunt people as their prey. This is particularly true in the Sunderban region of Bengal, India. This large area is made up of mangrove trees growing where three rivers meet the sea. People don't actually live there, but do visit to collect wood and hunt. However, tigers kill people there every year. Knowing that tigers like to sneak up on their prey, the wily locals started to wear masks on the back of their heads so a tiger creeping up from behind would think it had been spotted.

▲ FANCY A DIP?

Like pet cats, some big cats hate the water. Not the tiger though, which likes nothing better than a relaxing swim in a cool river or pond.

No two tigers have the same stripy pattern on their coats. Each tiger's coat is unique – a bit like your fingerprints.

Lions

The lion is often called the king of the beasts, and it's easy to see why. Although it's true that lions are not the biggest cats in the world, they are certainly kings of all they survey in their own territories. Lions used to be found in Africa, Asia and even Europe, but are now restricted to India and Africa.

▼ TEAM WORK ▲

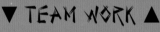

Lions are not the fastest of the big cats, which you would think might be a problem when hunting speedy gazelles or swift zebras. However, they get round this by hunting as a team. Generally, it's the lionesses that do all the hunting, but when it comes to eating it's the males who eat first – that doesn't really seem fair, does it?

▲ SOCIABLE CATS

Lions are social animals, which makes them something of a rarity in the cat world. They are the only cats to live in family groups, which are called prides. The head of the pride is the dominant male lion.

◀ SLIM PICKINGS

Even though lions are sociable, it's still a rough life for the cubs. They are always last to feed after a kill and it's not unknown for some cubs to starve to death if there's not enough meat to go round. Worse still, if a new lion becomes the pride's dominant male he is likely to kill the cubs of the old one.

Strangely, lion cubs are born with spots – as the cubs get older, the spots disappear.

◀ MANE ATTRACTION

Male lions are the only members of the cat family to have a mane. Nobody is exactly sure what it's for, but many scientists presume it's for making the lion look good and attracting lionesses. Interestingly, a recent study found that the darker the lion's mane, the more attractive the lion was to females.

Leopards

The leopard is one adaptable cat — it can live in all sorts of different environments and will hunt many types of animal, from lizards to baby giraffes. It is also the most widespread of the big cats and comes in a whole range of different sizes, depending on where it lives.

Some leopards' rosettes are a roundish shape and others are square, depending on where the leopard is from.

WHERE ARE THEY FOUND?

Leopards are found in Africa, India, Siberia, China and Indonesia. They can live in forests, grasslands, and even mountainous areas, depending on the country.

BLACK PANTHER ▶

Some leopards are born almost completely black in colour and are sometimes known as panthers. No one knows why this is, but there seem to be more panthers born in areas with thick jungles. Perhaps a dark coat would be even harder to see here. If you look closely at the coat you will see that it still has dark spots and rings, called rosettes.

▲ DIFFERENT VARIETIES

There are more than 20 species or subspecies of leopard, and they come in all sorts of shapes and sizes. In fact, some scientists believe that two sorts of leopard, the clouded leopard of the Indonesian islands and the snow leopard of Siberia, are different enough from normal leopards to be classed as a different species entirely.

▼ DISAPPEARING TRICK

A leopard's coat is covered in rosettes. This odd patterning is excellent for helping it hide in trees or long grass. In fact, the leopard is one of the stealthiest hunters on the planet and is expert at creeping right up on its prey without the unfortunate animal realizing.

▼ FOLLOW ME

Being so good at hiding does have its downside – it makes it very difficult for your cubs to find you or follow you in the grass. Leopards overcome this problem by having bright white patches behind their ears which the cubs find easy to spot.

▲ TREES

Leopards are great climbers and spend a lot of time up trees either sleeping or hunting. Trees serve another useful purpose – they're a great place for leopards to hide their food. After making a kill, leopards are anxious that some other predator, such as a lion, will steal it – so they carry the bodies into the trees for safe-keeping. This takes great strength, as sometimes a kill can weigh up to three times what the leopard weighs itself.

Cheetahs

The cheetah is the great specialist of the cat world and has developed into a lightning-fast hunting machine. But life is still pretty hard for cheetahs. Once they could be found throughout Africa, the Middle East and in India, but now these sleek, speedy animals are an endangered species.

Cheetahs have two large black lines running down their faces from their eyes, which make them look like they are crying.

WHERE ARE THEY FOUND?

It used to be thought that cheetahs could only hunt on the open plains of the African savannah but, in fact, cheetahs are also found in mountainous areas. There are cheetahs in many parts of Africa, and there may even be small population in Iran.

FAST CAT ▶

Cheetahs are not only the fastest of the big cats, they are the fastest land animal on the planet. These speedy cats can reach around 100 kilometres per hour, which is nearly as fast as cars can legally travel on the motorway. Such a talent for speed comes in handy when chasing lunch across the plains, but the cheetah can't run this fast for very long. Usually it will give up chasing after about 20 seconds, though sometimes a chase will last as long as a minute.

▲ SPEEDY BUT WEEDY

Extreme speed has its downsides, however. The cheetah is quite a light-weight cat, which is great for travelling fast, but bad for fighting. Often a cheetah will catch its prey, only to have it stolen by a bigger, meaner predator such as a lion, hyena or even a baboon. So, although cheetahs have a high hunting success rate compared to other big cats, they can still go hungry.

▲ ROYAL CONNECTIONS

Cheetahs are one of the easiest cats to tame and were once the fashionable pets of ancient royalty. In fact, it is believed the cheetahs have been caught as pets for over 5,000 years. The cheetahs were used as hunting cats by royalty from Sumeria to Europe, who used the cheetahs' awesome speed to catch other animals.

CHEEP! CHEEP!

Cheetahs don't roar, like some of the big cats. Instead, they make an odd little noise which sounds like chirping. When annoyed they hiss, and when happy cheetahs make a loud purring noise – just like a big tabby cat.

Cougars

The sleek and athletic cougar is the most widespread of American big cats. In some parts of America it is still legal to hunt these magnificent animals, though many people are trying to stop this.

WHERE ARE THEY FOUND?

Cougars are found from southern Canada right down to Patagonia in South America. However, their distribution is patchy, and many populations are becoming isolated by new housing developments blocking off the links between each area they inhabit.

▲ FACE TO FACE

Occasionally, people and cougars come face to face. If it happens to you, the trick is to make yourself look as big as possible and stare the cougar straight in the eye. If you're wearing a jacket, spread it out like a big cape behind you. Never bend down as this makes you look more like cougar food. Never take your eyes off the cougar and don't turn round.

◄ OH SO SECRET

Even though cougars live over such a huge area of both North and South America, very few people have actually seen them in the wild. There are a couple of reasons for this. Firstly, cougars hunt at dawn, dusk, and night so there are fewer people around at those times to see them. And secondly, cougars are very shy animals and will usually go out of their way to avoid people.

BURIED TREASURE ▶

Once a cougar has made a kill, it wants to keep hold of it. It cleverly buries its kill under a pile of leaves and dirt. With its food safely hidden, the cougar returns to it every night until it's all gone.

Cougars are called a variety of names including puma, mountain lion and Florida panther.

PAIN IN THE NECK ▶

Cougars aren't fussy eaters and will eat almost anything from deer to insects. Cougars like to sneak up on their prey in the same way other big cats do, and when their food is close by, the cougar pounces on it with one mighty leap. However, unlike other the big cats, a cougar doesn't strangle its prey but breaks its neck with a bite from its powerful jaws.

Jaguars

WHERE ARE THEY FOUND?

Jaguars are most common in forested areas of South and Central America, but they are also found in south-western parts of North America.

The greatest South American predator is the jaguar. Like the leopard, the jaguar is a stealthy night hunter, using its excellent night-vision to track prey. Like most big cats, the jaguar lives on its own and is an expert at hiding in the trees or bushes and, like leopards, some jaguars have black fur too.

▼ HEADACHE

Unlike most big cats, jaguars do not kill their prey by biting them around the neck and suffocating them. Instead, jaguars use their powerful jaws and sharp teeth to bite their prey in the head and kill them that way.

◀ GONE FISHING

Jaguars eat a wide range of animals from deer to crocodilians. Jaguars have also developed an ingenious method of fishing. The cat waits by the water and splashes the surface every so often with its tail. For some reason, this attracts fish which are promptly scooped out of the water with the jaguar's paws.

SPOT THE DIFFERENCE ▶

Jaguars are often confused with leopards, but they live on different continents and are a heavier and stockier cat. There is also a subtle difference to their spotty coats. Both jaguars and leopards have a spotty, rosette pattern, but it's the inside of the rosettes which give the game away – jaguars have a few smaller spots inside the rosettes, leopards don't.

Tribespeople often call the jaguar 'the beast which kills its prey with one bound'.

I CAN HEAR YOU

Jaguars are one of the few members of the cat family which can roar. The other big cats which roar are lions, tigers and the jaguars' close relatives, leopards.

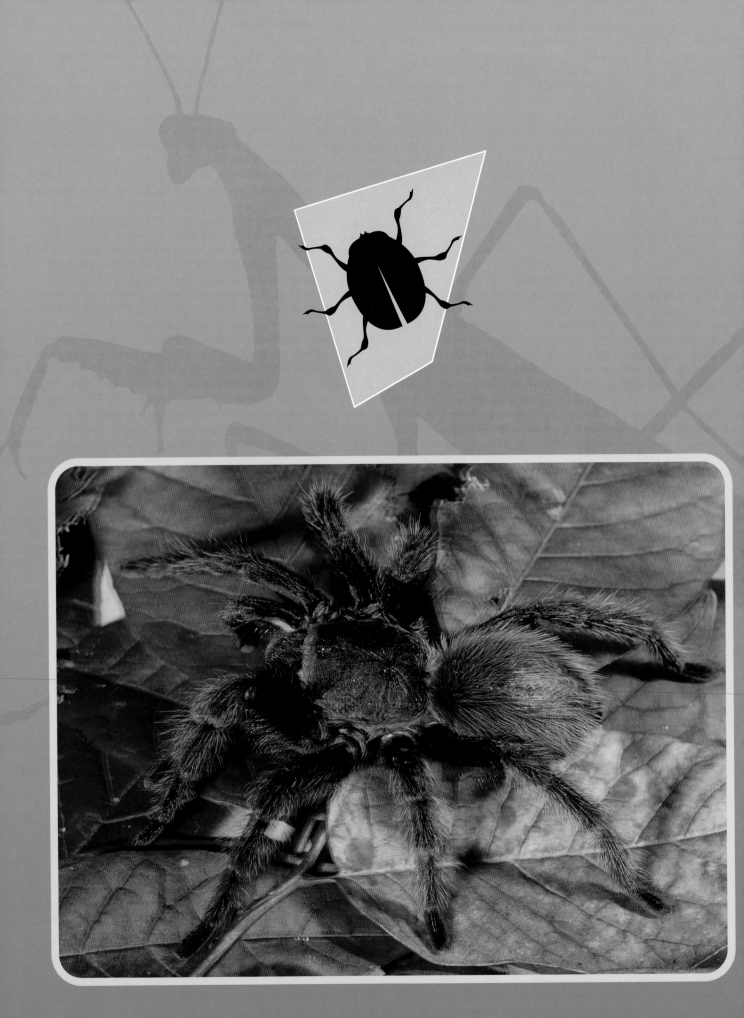

BUGS

What is a Bug?

Bugs, creepy crawlies, minibeasts...call them what you will, people don't seem to have a high opinion of these mini-marvels of the animal world. This is really unfair for many reasons, in fact — as you'll discover later — bugs are so useful that life on our planet depends on them. Like them or loathe them, it's guaranteed you'll be amazed by them.

There are more different species of insect in the world than any other type of animal.

BIG GROUP ▼

Often when people talk about bugs, they mean a group of animals called arthropods. This group includes insects, which are animals with three body parts and six legs – beetles, ants and wasps are all examples of insects. The arthropod group also includes arachnids, which are animals like spiders, and crustaceans such as wood lice.

SURVIVORS ▼

Cockroaches are the great survivors of the animal kingdom. They can withstand any temperature and will eat practically anything. They also have a tough body which makes them difficult to kill and they breed very quickly. This combination makes them the animal most likely to be around long after most others have disappeared.

▲ SLOW MOVERS

The loose term 'bug' can also include another group of creatures called gastropods. Most people call them slugs and snails.

▲ ROUND THE WORLD

Bugs are superbly adaptable, so no matter where you are in the world you are sure to find bugs there, too. You'll see bugs in forests, cities, in the air and under water. Bugs can cope with heat, so you'll find them in the desert, and they're good in the cold, too, so you can even find some of them at the poles.

BIG NUMBERS

How many bugs are there in the world? It's difficult to tell as there are new species being discovered all the time. Estimates can vary between 6 and 9 million different species, but some scientists put the figure as high as 30 million different species.

Senses

We humans find two eyes more than enough to get about with, but not spiders. These web-spinning wonders don't just have eight legs, they also have eight eyes!

Just like us, bugs can hear, see, taste, smell and feel things. But as bugs look very different from us, they also experience all these things in a different way, too.

EYE EYE ▼

Many bugs have what are called 'compound' eyes. Their eyes are made up of lots of little hexagonal shapes. Each hexagon sees a different bit of what is in front of the bug, and the bug's brain puts together all the little viewpoints like a jigsaw so it can see the big picture. The bigger a bug's eyes, the better they can see, so a dragonfly's gigantic eyes give it great sight.

TASTY ▼

It will come as no surprise that bugs use different bits of their bodies to taste with. Some bugs use their mouths like we do. Other bugs, such as some flies, use their feet, as do butterflies. Imagine standing in your food before eating it – that's the trouble with bugs, no table manners.

I CAN HEAR YOU ▲

Bugs don't have ears as we know them. Instead they hear with different parts of their bodies. Many insects have fine hairs on their bodies which pick up the tiny vibrations made by sound. This does not necessarily mean they can hear though. Crickets, however, can definitely can hear – they pick up sounds through small holes in their forelegs.

TOUCHY FEELY ▼

Some scientists believe that bugs with poor eyesight, such as bees, rely on the stalks on their heads, called antennae, to feel objects – and each other. Other bugs use the hairs on their bodies to feel movement.

WHAT A RACKET ▲

The familiar sound of grasshoppers is made by them rubbing their back legs against their forewings. Crickets and katydids (relatives of crickets) rub their forewings together. But not all animals produce noise this way. The Madagascan hissing cockroach, for example, makes a loud hiss when it expels air through tiny holes in its body. And the cicada flexes its body in and out to produce its famous click.

SNIFF SNIFF

Some bugs may also use their antennae to smell their food. It seems that antennae are used for different things by different bugs, depending on how they live.

Getting About

B ugs have developed different ways of getting around because they live in different environments. For example, there's no point having wings if you spend all your life underground. So whether it's the expert flying of the dragonfly, the slow slide of the slug or the frantic scurrying of ants, each method of getting about suits the way that particular bug lives.

SLIP-SLIDING ▶

Snails and slugs move in an incredible way, using their one long foot which they squeeze in and out to get along. The slimy trail they leave is called mucus, a substance which helps them to slide over rough or sharp ground without getting injured.

How can you tell millipedes and centipedes apart? Millipedes have four legs for every body segment, centipedes have only two.

HAVE WINGS, WILL TRAVEL ▶

The best way of covering long distances is to take to the air. This could be why many bugs have wings. And some bugs *really* get about. A desert locust can travel thousands of miles in its lifetime. However, the top travellers of the bug world must be the monarch butterflies – some fly from Mexico to Canada and back every year.

LOTS OF LEGS ▼

Most bugs have six legs, others have eight, which might seem enough for anybody. Not centipedes and millipedes though, which can usually have between 100 and 400 legs. It is believed that some species of millipede might have up to 750 legs. Just imagine having an itchy foot – you'd never work out which one it was.

▲ JUMP AROUND

Why bother to walk though when it's much quicker to jump? Many insects, such as froghoppers, can jump as it's a useful way of avoiding trouble or hunting for food. The king of the jumping world is the flea. They can jump over 100 times their own height – that would be like us jumping over the Washington Monument or the London Eye!

Good Enough To

Like all other animals, bugs spend much of their time looking for something to eat, and avoiding being eaten at the same time. It really is a matter of life and death — and some bugs go to surprising lengths to make sure they're still around at the end of the day.

Not all bugs want to hide, some are very bright colours - this usually tells other animals that the bug doesn't taste nice.

NASTY SURPRISE ▼

No web-building for the crab spider – this sneaky predator lies in wait inside flowers to ambush its prey. It doesn't just hide though; it can also change its colour to match the flower it's hiding in. Not all bugs have good eyesight, so the spider doesn't often go hungry.

▲ NOT A PRAYER

The easiest way to hunt is if you can get your prey to come to you. As many bugs spend their life on twigs and stalks, it makes sense that if you look like a plant it's going to be pretty easy to catch your food. The praying mantis is an expert at this, blending in perfectly with its surroundings, waiting to catch its prey.

Eat

HIDE AND SEEK ▶

Butterflies, moths and caterpillars are hiding experts. The aptly named dead leaf butterfly can fold its brightly coloured wings together, showing their dull undersides. Its wings are even leaf-shaped, too, to help the transformation.

▲ HERE I AM

A different approach to avoiding predators is to look like a bigger, fiercer animal. The hawk moth caterpillar has markings at its back end which look a bit like a snake. It waves this end around to give that it is a moving snake.

DROPPING OUT ▶

The trouble with being a bug is that you're generally snack-sized as far as many other animals are concerned. The best way not to get eaten is to look like something you wouldn't want to eat. And surely the giant swallowtail butterfly caterpillar wins the unappetising meal competition – it looks exactly like a bird dropping.

Ganging Up

Many bugs live in huge extended families called colonies. The advantages of living in a group are obvious. There are more of you to look for food, to help protect the home from attack, and look after the young bugs and eggs.

HIGH RISE HOME ▼

A big family needs a big house, and few bug houses come any bigger than a termite's mound. The mounds can be over 4 metres, and are built over the termites' nest which is buried under ground. The mound is made of dried mud, and protects the nest from overheating, or getting too cold, or from letting in too much rain.

ORDERED SOCIETY ▲

Bugs which live in big groups tend to be very well organized, with different types of bug doing different jobs. Bees are a good example of this. At the top of the pile is the queen who lays all the eggs. Next are the drones which mate with the queen. At the bottom of the pile are the worker bees which find all the nectar to make honey. Worker bees are also expected to feed the queen and the young bees, as well as protect the hive from attack. It's no fun being at the bottom of the pile.

◄ PLAYING IN THE WATER

You would think that the last place you would expect to find an ant would be on a river. However, if fire ants get flooded out of their home they think nothing of grouping together in a big cluster and floating down the river. They'll drift about until they land somewhere drier where they can make their new home.

Millions of termites can live in a single mound at the same time.

DEADLY SWARM ▼

Sometimes, bugs which normally live alone gather together in huge groups with devastating effect. Locusts, a large, flying plant-eater, are not much of a problem when they are by themselves. However, if a few locusts get together they can start giving off signals that might attract more and more locusts until hundreds of thousands of them appear. When this huge swarm gets hungry they can strip fields bare for miles around.

Helping Out

Bugs may be on the small side, but don't underestimate how useful they are. If there were no bugs in the world nothing else would survive — for a start, they pollinate flowers. They're also Mother Nature's rubbish disposal brigade. Dead plants, dead animals and even animal droppings are got rid of by these hard-working helpers.

Some American beekeepers rent their hives to fruit farmers who use the bees to pollinate their fruit trees.

▼ DIRTY JOB

One of the most important insects on the planet has one of the most unpleasant jobs to do. The dung beetle takes other animals' poo and uses it to lay its eggs in, or even eats it. This might sound disgusting, but if dung beetles didn't do it we'd all be buried under a huge mound of the stinky stuff in no time.

▲ GARDENER'S FRIEND

As we have already seen, some bugs eat other bugs. This is good news for gardeners, as it means they can help to protect their plants by encouraging friendly bugs to visit. Adult ladybirds can eat up to fifty plant-chomping aphids a day – good news for gardeners.

NEW NUTRIENTS ▲

Soil needs feeding as much as you or I do. Soil gets its food from nutrients found in rotting vegetation. Insects such as millipedes and many ground beetles are great at eating dead plants and leaves. When these insects have a poo, it's full of the dead plant nutrients which the soil finds so necessary.

BAD BUGS ▼

So why do bugs get a bad rap? Partly, it's down to fear – loads of people get a fright from a spider in the bath tub, for example. Also, it's because people don't like bugs doing what they do. Fleas, for example, need to feed on blood. But when that blood comes from a human or their pet, then the flea becomes public enemy number one. And finally some bugs, such as mosquitoes, can pass on harmful illnesses or diseases.

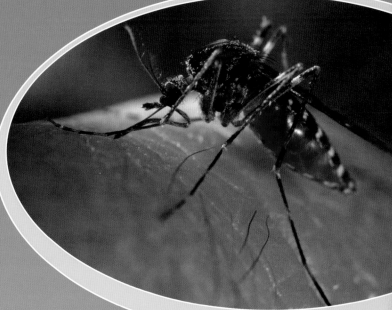

▼ NO MYSTERY

Ever wonder why you never see many dead birds or other dead wild animals? That's because dead creatures are a great source of food for beetles and maggots (which are baby flies). They can polish off a bird in just a few days.

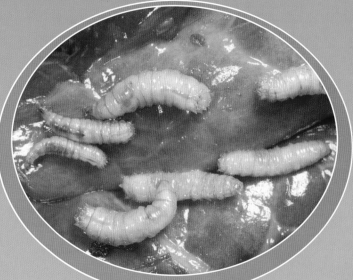

As there are so many bugs, it'll be no surprise to hear that they come in all sorts of shapes and sizes. Bugs can be so small you need a microscope to see them. Or they can be more than big enough to give you a nasty fright if you weren't expecting to see one.

There is evidence that up to a tenth of the weight of a 2 year-old pillow is made up of house dust mites and their droppings. Eeuurrgghh!

BIG BEETLE

The Goliath beetle is one of the longest – and certainly the heaviest – insect in the world. This giant bug is over 12 centimetres long and weighs about as much as an apple. It might look scary, but actually it's very useful as it eats dead plant material and animal poo.

▲ DRAGONFLIES

As well as being some of the most beautiful insects around, dragonflies and damselflies are also some of the biggest. Some of these colourful marvels can have wingspans approaching 20 centimetres in length. However, compared to their ancient relatives, this is tiny. During the time of the dinosaurs, some dragonflies had wingspans over 68 centimetres long.

Micro

▲ BIG SHELL

The giant African land snail's name is a bit of a giveaway – this huge gastropod is the largest snail in the world and can grow up to 20 centimetres long. You wouldn't want to find one of those crawling over your salad!

▲ TINY, BUT TROUBLE

We've all heard of animals being infected by insects such as fleas, but would you think that insects also get infected? Well, it happens, and sometimes with deadly effect. Honey bees can become infested by a microscopic mite called *Acarapis woodi*. It makes the adult bees unable to fly and lose their sense of direction. Bees that can't fly, can't find food, so the colony begins to die off.

▶ SHARING A BED

You probably haven't seen one of these in real life, but you've certainly slept with one! It's a house dust mite, and at less than 0.02 centimetres in length you'd need pretty good eyesight to spot it – even though your bed mattress could well be home to literally millions of them. These mites eat dead skin, so really they're doing a clean-up job for us.

Contributor credits:
3D glasses illustrator: Ian Thompson
3D images by Pinsharp 3D Graphics

Futher credits by chapter:

DINOSAURS
Author: Heather Amery
Picture credits: Ardea London Ltd; Discovery
Communications Inc; Natural History Museum (London).

SNAKES
Author: Paul Harrison
Picture credits: Nature Picture Library; NHPA; Science
Photo Library.

JUNGLE
Author: Paul Harrison
Picture credits: Jungle Photos; Nature Picture Library;
NHPA; FLPA; Still Pictures.

SHARKS
Authors: Lynn Gibbons and Chris Coode
Picture Credits: BBC; Planet Earth; Oxford Scientific Films.

T REX
Author: Paul Harrison
Picture credits: Ardea London Ltd; Natural History Museum
(London); Nature Picture Library; Oxford Scientific Science
Photo Library; (OSF)/Photolibrary.com; The Field Museum,
Chicago by John Weinstein.

REPTILES
Author: Paul Harrison
Picture credits: Nature Picture Library; NHPA; Oxford
Scientific (OSF)/Photolibrary.com; Science Photo Library;
John White Photos.

BIG CATS
Author: Paul Harrison
Picture credits: Ardea London Ltd; Bridgeman Art Library;
Nature Picture Library; NHPA; Oxford Scientific (OSF)/
Photolibrary.com; Science Photo Library.

BUGS
Author: Paul Harrison
Picture credits: FLPA; Nature Picture Library: NHPA; Oxford
Scientific (OSF)/Photolibrary.com.